MAKE A
DIFFERENCE

Following Your Passion and Finding Your Place to Serve

JAMES A. HARNISH

Leader Guide
by John P. Gilbert

Abingdon Press / Nashville

MAKE A DIFFERENCE
FOLLOWING YOUR PASSION AND
FINDING YOUR PLACE TO SERVE
LEADER GUIDE

This book is printed on elemental chlorine-free paper.
ISBN 978-1-5018-47608

17 18 19 20 21 22 23 24 25 26 — 10 9 8 7 6 5 4 3 2 1
MANUFACTURED IN THE UNITED STATES OF AMERICA

CONTENTS

SOME SUGGESTIONS FOR LEADING THIS STUDY

Every day we see that things are not right in our world, and as followers of Jesus Christ, we have an impulse to do something about it. We long to connect our passions and gifts with the needs around us, making a unique contribution for the healing of the world.

In this study of *Make a Difference*, by James A. Harnish, you will begin to answer the questions "How can I become a part of God's healing work in this world?" and "How can I find my place to serve and make a difference?" Through the book, video, and your own group conversations, you will explore biblical wisdom and the stories of real people who have found their place to serve, making God's kingdom a reality in this life. You and your fellow group members will help one another discover how God is calling each of you to work for the transformation of the world.

It's important to realize that in this particular situation, you are not teaching in a traditional sense. In other words, you are not imparting knowledge that the members of your group may not have, and you are not trying to help folks master particular facts or skills. Instead, in this study, think of yourself as a guide or even as a fellow traveler. You are a facilitator, one who helps others look inside themselves, deep within themselves, to discover and employ God's call on their lives. You'll look inside yourself as well to hear God's call for you. And together with your fellow group members, you'll discover how to utilize what you already know or have learned about God's direction for your lives.

It won't be an easy task, certainly not as easy as teaching facts. But in many ways it will be far more rewarding, because you'll experience growth yourself as you learn with others how God is calling you to make a difference too.

On the following pages, you will find a few practical suggestions for gathering and guiding your group.

Group Size

Keep the group small. This is not a lecture to a crowd; this is helping persons plumb the depths of their commitment to God's will for their lives. Six to twelve participants is ideal. If you have more than twelve persons, consider dividing the group into two or more subgroups of six. You can all still gather at the same time to meet, view the video, and discuss things in the larger group. But the subgroups of six will allow for deeper, more focused discussion at several points where it will be appreciated.

If you do choose to break into smaller clusters, be sure each group member, including you, is included in a cluster. You are not one who stands afar and tells everyone else what to do; you are also a full member of and an active part of the whole group and one of the smaller clusters. You might also encourage a wife and husband to be members of different subgroups. Think how enriching the conversations on the way home will be when wives and husbands are in different groups!

Finally, although taking such a position is difficult, "close" the group no later than the second of the six sessions. The sessions build one on another, and if people choose to join the group for the last two or three sessions, it will be disruptive for everyone. If people can't make the first two sessions, offer the study again in a month or six weeks so that they can have another opportunity to participate!

Supplies and Equipment

The book *Make a Difference: Following Your Passion and Finding Your Place to Serve* by James A. Harnish. Be sure that each participant has a copy of this book at least one week before your first session. Ask each participant to read the introduction and chapter 1, "Awakening!" prior to your first session. Yes, it's fine to underline, highlight, or write marginal notes in the book. Remind group members to bring their study books and their personal Bibles to each session.

Refreshments. Something to snack on is always welcome, but keep it simple. A table of light refreshments, some sweet and some salty, is all you need. Ask group members to take turns providing refreshments, but remind them that this is not the place for one-upmanship or a cake-baking contest. Simple snacks will be easy for people to provide and will not distract from your main purpose of meeting together. Invite folks to grab some refreshments as they arrive and to get refills as needed. Encourage participants to bring their own drinks in order to avoid the hassles of making coffee and tea (hot or iced) and guessing who likes what sodas or fruit juices.

A candle and matches or lighter. Each time you meet, you'll begin by lighting a candle in honor of someone who has made a positive, God-shaped difference in your life. So be sure to provide a candle and matches or a lighter each week for your group. A simple pillar or votive candle is perfect for this.

Markerboard and markers. A large surface to record your group's ideas is always useful. A markerboard is suggested, but a chalkboard or large pad of paper will work as well. If you need to divide the group into smaller subgroups (see "Group Size," above), be sure that each group has a surface to write on and writing instruments.

DVD Player. Because this is a video-based study, a DVD player (or computer) and large-screen television or projector and screen is critical. Be sure you have the appropriate cords and connectors to play the DVD. It's always a good idea to test the arrangement beforehand just to make certain.

Bibles. Have a number of Bibles in various translations (CEB, RSV, NRSV, NIV, TEV, for example) available, but also encourage participants to bring their own Bibles to each session.

Paper, pencils, and pens. Be sure that there's enough paper and pencils or pens for each person to write down key thoughts and ideas. Or encourage each person to bring a notebook of his or her own to take notes.

Other supplies. Check the "Prepare" section for each session in this Leader Guide for other specific supplies that may be needed for a given session.

Meeting Space and Time

Room arrangement can be important. Don't meet in the pews in the sanctuary unless it's absolutely necessary. A meeting space that will allow your whole group to meet in circles around a table will be ideal—or a space with multiple such arrangements if you have a larger group breaking down into smaller clusters. A circle of chairs or chairs arranged around a small table allows everyone to be seen and heard. It tends to quiet the folks who talk a lot, and it helps give the timid participants a chance to be heard in a supportive context.

How long should sessions last? This Leader Guide assumes a session time of sixty minutes, but you should feel free to adapt based on your group's needs. If you have more time each week to meet, you can easily plan on spending more time in discussion to extend your session to ninety minutes. Here's an extra time-related hint: always start on time and end on time, regardless of who is or is not present. This will ensure that your group's participants will arrive on time, and it will show everyone that you respect their schedules. You'll all make the most out of your time together.

Your Own Preparation

First, of course, surround yourself with prayer. Pray for each participant by name before and after each session. Pray for God's direction and inspiration as you prepare to lead each session.

Always begin and end each session with a group prayer, but share the offering of these prayers with the group members.

Read the coming chapter and biblical references as early in the week as you can. The day after each session is the right time to begin preparing for the next session. In addition, read the session plan in the Leader Guide several days in advance to prepare for your meeting and gather any necessary supplies. View the video component as well, and make notes on key points that stand out. Let both the contents of the chapter and the biblical readings "percolate" in your mind as you go about your regular activities. Don't hesitate to consult biblical commentaries and your pastor to clarify some ideas and concepts, if you feel that it's necessary.

But always, always keep in mind that you are a fellow participant, a learner alongside the other group members. You are not the "professor" or the answer person; you are not the judge or arbiter of right or wrong responses from the group members. You are a learner with them. Ask God to speak to each of you, so that you may discover God's will for your lives and see how you are being called to make a difference.

Session 1

AWAKENING!

Overview

This first session is very personal, as are all the sessions in this study. No one can read the first chapter in *Make a Difference* without being moved, challenged, and—to use an old word—convicted. With this in mind, the primary objectives of this session for each participant and for your group are:

- to become acquainted with one another on a level perhaps deeper than what you have encountered before. Most of the persons in your group (or groups) may know one another casually, informally, or socially, but this study will lead persons to meet and come to know one another on a much deeper and therefore more significant basis.
- to enter into serious self-examination and reflection. This will be personal for each participant; it will be profound and perhaps at times a bit threatening. But the end results of

this reflection will be a deeper commitment to Christ and a renewed dedication to serving Christ and others, making a unique difference in the world.

- to explore biblical passages that spoke not just to the people of two or three thousand years ago but also to us today in our own times and places with an unmistakable clarion call.

- to begin to realize that God's call to service is universal; that is, the call is to all, not just to some. God calls each of us to find the unique place and way to serve, regardless of our place in society and the world.

- to take the initial steps of hearing and responding to the call of Christ—not in a broad and general way but in a very direct and personal way. Of course, one of the overall goals of the entire study is the hearing, clarifying, and responding to God's call to discipleship, service, and witness.

Prepare

Before your meeting, carefully read through chapter 1 in *Make a Difference*, and make a list of the key biblical references discussed by the author, James Harnish. Don't worry about listing every Bible verse cited; just the ones that seem important to you as you read the chapter. List these references by book, chapter, and verse only, then make as many copies of the list as there will be participants. Have these lists ready to hand out at the appropriate time in the session.

Set up the meeting room so that all can see the television monitor or projector screen. If your group is large enough to need to divide into smaller clusters of six or so persons, arrange space for these clusters around small tables if possible.

Provide a candle, candle holder, and a means for lighting the candle for the group (or for each smaller cluster). Your group will light the candle at this first session, following the viewing of the DVD, and will light the candles at the beginning of each succeeding session.

Welcome participants as they arrive, and invite the participants to visit the refreshment table and to bring their refreshments to the table and chairs.

Welcome and Opening Prayer

At the time appointed to begin, do so by welcoming the participants all together. Briefly explain that each of your meeting sessions will involve some personal sharing, and therefore that mutual respect and confidentiality are imperative. Commence the session with this or another appropriate prayer:

Almighty God, you summon each of us to a life of service, of sacrifice if need be, and of the perfect joy that comes from living according to your will. We seek to discover your will for our lives—not in general terms but in the specific ways you have summoned each one of us, for we believe you indeed have a task for each of us. Bless our conversations, bless our meditations, and bless the decisions and the directions with which we emerge from this study together. We ask all of this in the name of the Christ who taught us to pray: Our Father. Who art in heaven...

Continue with the Lord's Prayer.

Introductions

Begin this session by inviting each participant to introduce herself or himself. This introduction should include something of each person's faith background, of the individual's present involvement in the church, and, most important, why the individual chose to become part of this study group. Allow time for the others in the group to ask questions for clarification of the one sharing, but these questions should not be challenging or argumentative.

Note: Do note rush this process and do not allow a participant to "toss off" the question by saying, for example, "You all know me..." Details of work life, of extended family, of hobbies or other interests are not as important as one's faith journey and one's sense of need to grow in service and discipleship.

Ask: Why do you want to make a difference? How do you hope God will speak to you personally through this study?

View the Video

Introduce the video, reminding the group that they will view a discussion between the author, James Harnish, and four conversation partners. For reference, the video panel members are listed on pages 7–8 of *Make a Difference*. Invite the group members to take notes on the video session, jotting down questions or comments that arose in their minds as they watched. Before beginning the video, indicate to the group members that anyone can ask to have parts of it repeated if he or she needs to clarify something. For example, anyone may say something like, "Wait, back it up a bit. I didn't quite catch what he was saying there."

The video begins with a brief candle lighting, with Rev. Harnish lighting a candle in honor of an important person who made a difference in his life. After your group views the video, explain to the group that you'll begin each session by lighting a candle as well. Name a person who has made a difference in your life, and explain briefly why that person has been important to you. Light the candle in his or her honor. Explain to the group that in your next session, another person will have the opportunity to light the candle in honor of someone.

After lighting the candle, discuss the video.

Ask: What key insights stood out to you in the conversation we just watched? How do they help you see what it means to wake up?

Ask: The speakers in the video mentioned places of disruption. Why are places of disruption so important? How can we hear God's call in those places?

Ask: Lisa mentioned the relationship between what we do and who we are. How does our identity shape what we are called to do?

On newsprint or a markerboard, write down these questions so that you can keep them in mind and address them in this or a future session.

Engage

Invite each participant to share one key insight from the introduction or from chapter 1, "Awakening!" in *Make a Difference.*

Ask: How did the introduction and first chapter of *Make a Difference* challenge you? How did it make you uncomfortable? Why?

Reverend Harnish uses the image of being asleep in this chapter— both humorously as in sleeping during sermons and very seriously as in being asleep to the claim that Christ makes on each of us. As a group, discuss some of the factors that keep us "asleep" to God's call and claim on our lives. As the leader, encourage everyone to think in specific, personal terms as well as in more general terms as you discuss one or more of the following questions:

Ask: What are some things that cause us to fall asleep to God's call, or to stay asleep?

Ask: Have you ever hit the "snooze button" on God's call? In what ways do you think of God's claim on you as something that you will "get around to doing someday"?

Ask: What in our contemporary world makes us unable to see or hear the claim God makes upon us?

Ask: What makes us resist God's claim on our lives?

Ask: If we were to be serious about responding to God's claim on us, what might we have to surrender, to give up, in order to hear God?

Ask: What will need to change in your life for you to awaken and respond enthusiastically to God's summons?

Remember Who You Are

Read aloud the following quotation from chapter 1 of *Make a Difference*, where author James Harnish writes, "We can stay awake to God's calling by constantly remembering who we really are" (page 27).

Ask: When did you last think of your baptism or your confirmation? What responsibilities came with that?

Ask: How does being a Christian shape your identity? How does it shape your behavior and your commitments?

Ask: How does knowing that you are loved—unconditionally loved by God—change your understanding of God's calling on your life? What motivates you to respond to God's call in that case?

Reclaim Your Mission

Distribute the list of Scripture passages discussed in this chapter (see "Prepare," above). Assign a passage from the list to each person in the group, recognizing that some people may need to be given two Scripture passages. Ask one person to read aloud his or her passage, then discuss the following questions:

- What does this passage communicate about the mission of Jesus Christ, of the church, or of individual disciples?
- What would it look like for us to participate in that mission? What specific actions might it lead to in our community or beyond?

After the group has responded to these questions, ask the next person to read aloud his or her passage and discuss the same questions again. Repeat until each person has read his or her passage.

Ask: How does recognizing our mission as disciples of Jesus help us come more fully awake to God's call on us individually?

Renew Your Vision

James Harnish shares a number of interesting stories of those who have heard and responded to God's call in the first chapter of *Make a Difference* and in the video conversation. Keeping these stories and others like it in mind can help us to renew our vision, to "keep our eyes on the prize" and stay awake to God's calling. Invite the group to identify some of those stories and discuss which stories had a special effect on some or all of the participants.

> **Say:** On page 34 of *Make a Difference*, the author writes, "We can keep our eyes open for ordinary people who, in small and seemingly insignificant ways, demonstrate God's vision of the Kingdom in their life of servanthood." He shares a number of stories about such people in the first chapter and in the first video session.

> **Ask:** Which of these stories stood out to you as being especially powerful? Why?

> **Ask:** How do these stories inspire you to stay awake to God's call?

Next, invite the participants to share other stories they have read or heard that illustrate a commitment to responding to God's call to obedience and service.

> **Ask:** What other people have you encountered who have demonstrated a commitment to hearing and responding to God's call?

Note that these stories need not all have a Christian slant; God is God of the entire creation and some members of other faith communities demonstrate that total obedience to God's summons. But do not limit examples of obedience to God's call to famous persons; within each community are persons who exemplify hearing and responding to God's summons to awaken and serve.

Ask: What insights into responding to God's claim do these stories provide?

Ask: Considering all these examples, what difference have these persons made in the world around them?

Take Action

As you begin to conclude your session, give each person a piece of paper and something to write with. Invite each person to write down a response to two questions on the piece of paper—for that person's eyes only.

1. What is keeping me from responding fully to God's claim on me as a servant and living witness to Christ's kingdom?
2. What steps can I take to awaken and totally live out God's summons to discipleship and service?

After everyone has responded individually, ask the group to consider the "Action Ideas" for chapter 1, found on pages 40–41 of *Make a Difference*. Read these action ideas together, then invite each participant to indicate which action idea(s) she or he intends to incorporate into his or her life in the coming week.

Close the Session

Use the historic prayer from Wesley's Covenant Service to close this and each session:

Lord, make me what you will.
I put myself fully into your hands;
 put me to doing, put me to suffering,

let me be employed for you, or laid aside for you,
let me be full, let me be empty,
let me have all things, let me have nothing.
I freely and with a willing heart
give it all to your pleasure and disposal.[1]

---

1 "Wesley's Covenant Service," *The United Methodist Book of Worship* (Nashville: The United Methodist Publishing House, 2016), 291.

Session 2

WHO ARE THESE PEOPLE?

Overview

In this chapter of *Make a Difference*, James Harnish describes several persons who have lived out Albert Schweitzer's description of truly happy people—those who have learned that pure happiness comes through joyful service. But more than just providing vignettes of some remarkable people, the author challenges each one of us to be one of those who discovers blessing and wholeness through service. Thus, one of the goals of this chapter and the learning session based on this chapter is to identify what has made these persons who and what they are and what makes others like these persons—all with an eye toward stimulating within each participant a sense of "I want what these people have, and I want to find it as they did, through service." This, then, is a time for sharing stories of those who serve in both great and small ways, and for seeking whatever might be necessary to enable each participant in the study group to discover the same joy and fulfillment through service.

Prepare

Equip yourself by reading and annotating chapter 2 of *Make a Difference*, previewing the video, praying for your fellow participants, and asking for God's guidance as you lead the group this week. Arrive at your meeting place well before the time for the session to begin. This will enable you to give attention to details such as these:

- Be sure the chairs are in place, preferably around a table big enough to accommodate everyone in the group.
- Ensure that the television monitor and DVD player are in place and operating and that the remote controls work (it's a good idea to have a couple of extra batteries for the remote controls, just in case).
- Check on the availability of Bibles for participants to use. Be sure to have a variety of translations on hand.
- Provide a supply of paper and pens or pencils for participants to write with.
- Be sure that the markerboard or other writing surface is ready with appropriate markers.
- Bring a candle and a means to light it. This candle-lighting will be a part of each of these sessions.
- Prepare the refreshment table, with napkins, plastic silverware if needed, small paper plates, and so on.

Welcome and Opening Prayer

Welcome participants as they arrive. Invite them to help themselves at the refreshment table, then to join the group in your chairs or at the table.

Open the session with prayer. You might ask a participant in advance to be ready to begin the session with prayer, you may offer the opening prayer, or you could use a printed prayer from *The United Methodist Hymnal* or another source. However, personal prayers are often preferable to "read" prayers, so don't depend entirely on printed prayers.

Remind the group that you'll begin each session by lighting a candle in honor of someone who has made a difference in a group member's life. Invite a volunteer to name someone and light the candle in that person's honor.

View the Video

After lighting the candle, play the video of session 2 of *Make a Difference*. Remind participants that they can ask to replay a portion for clarification if necessary. Discuss the video by asking one or more of the following questions:

Ask: What did you hear in the video that seems especially important as you think about how to find your way to serve?

Ask: What did the speakers in the video see as the role of spiritual disciplines in a life of service?

Ask: Several of the speakers mentioned paying attention to what's in front of you, or even what you love to do. What opportunities to serve do you see in front of you right now?

Engage

Give each group member a piece of paper and something to write with. Invite each person to write down—for her or his eyes only—the following two self-descriptors:

1. Jot down in what ways you are a light to the world, beginning with your own community.
2. Describe the ways you are staying connected to God through prayer, Bible reading, and fellowship with other Christians.

When everyone has written something, help the group members understand that if their responses are incomplete, God may be nudging them through this study, and in other ways, to open themselves to service in the world. That nudging takes many forms; invite a few volunteers to describe for the whole group their experiences of nudging—times when they have felt God leading them in a particular direction.

Invite one or more volunteers to summarize the stories of Becca Stevens and Margaret Palmer from chapter 2 of *Make a Difference*. Ask each participant to respond to these stories by filling in the blank in the statement below, then discuss briefly their responses.

Fill in the blank:
That's great for Becca Stevens and Margaret Palmer! But I couldn't do something like that because _____.

Next, ask each participant to take turns filling in the blank in the following statement:

Fill in the blank:
Margaret Palmer and Becca Stevens inspire me to _____.

Finally, ask each participant to take turns filling in the blank below:

Fill in the blank:
I may be no Becca Stevens or Margaret Palmer, but what I can do is

_____.

Say: Many of us may not be able to do what Becca Stevens and Margaret Palmer did, for a variety of good reasons, but each of us can reflect the light of Christ in countless small ways every day. Service for Christ need not be grandiose or complicated, but it can be in the simplest acts.

Ask: What are some of the small ways you have found happiness through simple service that nevertheless made a difference?

Ask: When have you been the recipient of someone else reflecting the light of Christ in a simple way?

Ask: In what ways is the light of Christ reflected not only in grand service but in a willingness to spot even a simple need and react joyfully?

Start Small

Invite a volunteer to read John 6:1-13, the story of Jesus feeding five thousand people.

Ask: What did the boy who gave his lunch contribute? Was this gift beyond the boy's capacity to give it? Who is responsible for the great effect it had in Jesus' hands?

Invite a second volunteer to read Luke 10:25-37, the story of the good Samaritan.

Ask: What was so remarkable about the Samaritan who helped the injured man in this story? In what ways did he go above and beyond, and in what ways did he simply respond to a need he saw in front of him?

Ask: What do these two biblical examples teach us about our own opportunities for finding great joy and meaning in serving others?

Say: When we serve in seemingly insignificant ways, it invariably leads to opportunities to serve Christ and others in difficult or even time-consuming ways.

Ask: Consider again Becca Stevens and Margaret Palmer. In what ways did they start small and discover further opportunities to serve?

Ask: Do you think they receive greater joy now than they did before, because their ways of serving occur on a larger scale? Why or why not?

Ask: Do you know others who began small and found joy in serving? Has this taken place in your life at any time?

Ask: What have you witnessed God do with these small steps of service? How have they been rewarded with joy for the one who serves?

Stay Connected to the Power Source

A major theme of this chapter goes under the catchy title, "Stay Connected to the Power Source." Remind the group of this part of the chapter, and invite them to turn to pages 50–51 in *Make a Difference* for reference.

Ask: What is the power source Harnish describes, and how does one stay connected to that power source?

Ask: How is your connection to the power source? How often are you aware of this connection, and how strong does it feel?

Ask: Prayer is a key way to stay connected to the power source. How is your prayer life? When do you pray? What resources, if any, do you use when praying?

Ask: What experiences of answered prayer can you share? When have you experienced seemingly unanswered prayer?

Ask: What other ways does Harnish lift up our staying connected to the power source in all of life? How are these spiritual practices a part of your life?

Ask: How do you know if and when you are connected to God, whether through prayer or through these other means?

Say: Take heart. Trust that the power source of prayer is present when you pray for others, and the power source of prayer is present when others pray for you.

Take Action

Invite each group member to turn to the "Questions for Reflection" on page 59 of *Make a Difference*. Allow the group to read and think on these questions silently for five minutes, and to read over the "Action Ideas" on page 60.

Invite each participant to identify which action idea(s) he or she will commit to over the next week. As each person speaks, affirm him or her in the decision, and commit to praying for that person to experience a powerful connection to the power source and find joy in serving others. This selection is highly personal; try not to allow discussion except for clarification.

Close the Session

Invite each group member to write down at least one positive way she or he will strive to connect to the power source through prayer in the coming week, which may or may not be identical to the action idea he or she chose.

In the study book this chapter ends with a classic hymn, "Master, Speak." While this hymn is not in *The United Methodist Hymnal* at present, you may find the music in another hymnal. If so, ask the whole group to join in singing this hymn. If the music is not available, or if no one in the group can lead the participants in this hymn, invite the group members to join you in reading the words of this hymn aloud. Remind the group members that the first line of the first verse is taken from Eli's instructions to the boy Samuel, awakened at night by the Lord's summons. See 1 Samuel 3:1-10.

Then dismiss the participants by lining out the Wesley Covenant Prayer, pages 19-20 of this Leader Guide. "Lining out" simply means you will read a line aloud, then the participants will repeat the line after you.

Session 3

CHILDREN, GO WHERE
I SEND YOU

Overview

During this session, you will examine the ways in which group members hear God calling and the way they experience God equipping them to answer that call. Along the way, you will identify and face some of the most common excuses people—including perhaps yourself or your fellow group members—use for leaving their discipleship in the sanctuaries of the church and limiting their discipleship to one or two hours on Sunday mornings.

Prepare

Are you continuing to pray for your fellow participants in this study? Are you praying for each one by name, and do you know each one sufficiently to offer a very personal prayer for each? Are you praying as you prepare to lead each session, trusting God to guide you as you plan and execute your plan? And are you attuned to God's presence enough that you would happily abandon your plan in order to respond to the Lord's prompting?

Practically speaking, be sure to preview the video before the session, including taking careful notes and identifying portions you'd like the group to spend time discussing.

Arrive at your meeting place in plenty of time to arrange the chairs and table(s) in preparation for your meeting. Be sure the television and DVD player (including the remote control) are in place and operational. Arrange the refreshment table, set up the markerboard or other writing surface, check on the assortment of Bibles of several translations, and be sure that paper and pens or pencils are available for each group member. Finally, ensure that the group's candle and a means of lighting it are ready to begin your session.

One bit of special preparation you will need for this session is to choose a spiritual gifts assessment tool. You will encourage your fellow group members to complete a spiritual gifts assessment at home during the coming week, with plans to discuss it at your next session. Choose one of the two online spiritual gifts assessment tools available at the following websites and provide the web address to your fellow group members:

- https://www.umcdiscipleship.org/new-church-starts /spiritual-gifts
- http://www.umc.org/what-we-believe/spiritual-gifts -online-assessment

As you have before each of these sessions, find a quiet place where you can pray for God's presence with you as you lead this session.

Then greet participants as they arrive and invite them to the refreshment table. Get ready to lead the session when all have arrived, but remember that it is better to commence the session on the agreed-upon time even if some participants have not yet arrived.

Welcome and Opening Prayer

When everyone has arrived, invite all to join in a time of silent prayer. Make this an extended time, not just a moment or two. Then offer this or a similar prayer in the name of the whole group:

Lord, you who call each of us in the midst of the routine and busyness of our lives, you who call each of us to lives, actions, and deeds of genuine discipleship: Open our eyes to see the faces of those in need around us. Open our ears to hear the cries of the needy around the world and in our own community. Convict us and show us the ways you would have us serve you by serving our sisters and brothers. In the name of the Master Servant, Christ Jesus, we pray. Amen.

Invite a volunteer to light the group's candle in honor of someone who has made a difference in his or her life. Ideally, every participant will have an opportunity to do this before the study has completed. If you have more than six participants, suggest to the group that two or more people might wish to pair up and lift up the same person or group of people this time or next time.

View the Video

After you have lit the candle, view the video for session 3 of *Make a Difference*. As always, be prepared to stop the video or to replay a segment at the request of a group member. After watching the video, invite the group to discuss the following questions:

Ask: How does the video conversation clarify the idea that the church is not a building but instead is the work in the world of those committed to Christ?

Ask: In the video, Jim and Nick talk about stopping, ceasing activity, as a countercultural thing. Do you agree with them? What new possibilities does stopping open up for us?

Ask: Lisa talks about the need to see differently. Who or what might you need to see differently in order to find your place to serve?

Engage

Invite the group participants to compete with one another briefly. Give each person a piece of paper and a pen or pencil, then say:

Harnish contrasts "spinning," riding a stationary bicycle in an air-conditioned gym, with pedaling a bicycle outdoors on the open road. List as many ways of "spinning" in our Christian lives—staying comfortably in our churches—as you can identify in one minute. Go!

Time the group using a phone or watch, and call time at the end of one minute. Ask for totals from each member, and let the person with the most examples of Christian "spinning" read his or her list aloud. Invite the other participants to add other examples from their lists.

Invite a participant to summarize the amusing and fictional story of Gert from chapter 3 (see *Make a Difference* page 61).

Say: Harnish uses this tale to emphasize the reality that discipleship may begin in church on Sunday morning, but that discipleship is always lived out in the world every day.

Invite a volunteer to read Micah 6:8, and then ask a second volunteer to read Matthew 22:36-40.

> **Ask:** How do these two passages—one from the Old Testament and one from the New Testament—point those who would believe toward a life of active discipleship?

> **Ask:** How do you personally rate yourself in living out discipleship as described by these two passages? How would you rate our church? Why?

Explore Examples from the Scriptures and the Church

On pages 63–64 of *Make a Difference*, Harnish lists seven examples from the Scriptures, and one from The United Methodist denomination, that call persons to engage in continuous acts of discipleship and service in the world.

Assign one of the seven scriptural examples to each group member, and invite that person to read her or his example and to describe how that example can be put into practice here and now, starting in the immediate community and extending worldwide. (If you have fewer than eight participants, assign two examples to one or more persons.)

Note that the eighth example in the list concerns a statement of mission of The United Methodist Church. Ask a volunteer to read that statement, then discuss with one or more of the following questions.

> **Ask:** What is the meaning of the phrase "the transformation of the world"?

> **Ask:** Is such a transformation possible? Why or why not? Where and how does such a transformation begin?

Ask: How do the passages considered earlier from Micah and Matthew help define and describe the transformation of the world?

Ask: How do individual Christians and Christian communities determine what transformation should look like? How do we know what should be transformed? How do we know what it should be transformed into?

Come unto Me

Recall for the group the image of Christ with outstretched arms and the phrase "Come unto Me," first over the chancel of a church and then over the main exit door of the church (see *Make a Difference* page 65).

Say: Some churches print these sentences in the Sunday worship bulletin following the benediction: "Our service of worship has ended. Our worship through service begins."

Ask: How is our congregation emphasizing our need to be seeking places to serve throughout the week? What do we do in worship or in other ways to communicate this need to one another? How do you feel about this emphasis?

Spiritual Gifts Assessment

Before you close the session, inform the group about the spiritual gifts assessment available at one of the following websites:

- https://www.umcdiscipleship.org/new-church-starts /spiritual-gifts

- http://www.umc.org/what-we-believe/spiritual-gifts
  -online-assessment

Challenge each group member to complete this assessment carefully and prayerfully in the quiet of his or her own home, encouraging them to be as honest as possible in responding to each question.

Invite participants to print or otherwise record the results of their spiritual gifts assessments and bring them to your next session, ready to discuss their findings. Assure all that these discussions will be held in confidence by all group members.

Take Action

Remind the group about Harnish's emphasis in this chapter on the railroad crossing admonishment to stop, look, and listen. Invite each participant to share with the group at least one time he or she has been *stopped* by an opportunity to serve beyond the church building, or a time she or he has *looked* and seen clearly an opportunity outside of church to serve, or an instance in which he or she has *listened* and heard a call to serve beyond the church.

Call the group's attention to the "Action Ideas" on page 84 of *Make a Difference*. Encourage the group to review these silently, reflecting on how one or more of these ideas can help them to stop, look, and listen for God's call amid the needs of the world around them.

Invite each person to identify a specific action idea that he or she can implement over the coming week and write it down. Suggest that each participant keep the note that he or she has written in a purse or wallet and refer to that note at least three times each day—upon arising, at midday, and before retiring for the night.

Close the Session

Invite the participants in this study to a time of silent prayer in which they will pray quietly for the things that you will call out. Give the participants several moments to pray for each of the concerns you mention. These are the concerns to call out:

1. Pray for yourself, for whatever need you are feeling right now
2. Pray that you might stop, look, and listen to God's call and claim on your life.
3. Pray that you might have the courage to respond to that call, truly believing that God has a claim on the life God has given you.
4. Pray for your local church, that it might equip you in every way to bear the good news of the gospel wherever you might be.
5. Offer a genuine prayer of thanksgiving that God loves you, forgives you, hears your prayers, and equips you for service in your family, in your church, in your community, and in the world.

Harnish uses a prayer attributed to St. Francis of Assisi to end this chapter. Invite your group to read that prayer aloud together as printed on page 83 of *Make a Difference*.

GO TOGETHER

Overview

This session focuses on the fact that mission and discipleship are multiplied many times over by the involvement of others. To use a popular cliché, there are no "Lone Rangers" in service and mission. Active, genuine discipleship is never solitary. This reality is supported by the Scriptures, both the Old and the New Testaments, and by the history of the church over two thousand years. Thus, this chapter addresses how to find and enlist support (or how it can be found and enlisted by another). When any of us takes up the daunting task of making a difference for good in the world, we quickly discover that we cannot do it alone. God intends for us to journey with others toward the goals of justice, peace, reconciliation, and the transformation of the world. Indeed, while Jesus Christ was unique and an individual, he still recruited the Twelve in addition to the crowds that followed him and hung on his every word. Could Jesus have accomplished his ends alone? We may not be able to answer that definitively, but we do have the clarion example of his active recruitment of others. In this session, we'll explore the benefits of going together with other disciples as we seek to make a Kingdom-shaped difference in our world.

Prepare

Prepare for this session as you have for the preceding sessions: read chapter 4 of *Make a Difference* and make ample notes, then preview the video and identify key points that stand out for you. Review the lesson plan below. And be sure to pray for your fellow group members, as well as to ask for God's guidance as you lead the conversation this week. Arrive at the meeting place in plenty of time to take care of any housekeeping matters, such as:

- arranging furniture as needed;
- making sure that the DVD player and television monitor are in working order. (You have previewed the DVD for this session, haven't you?);
- setting up the refreshment table with needed utensils and paper goods (plates, cups, plastic silverware as needed);
- making the markerboard or other writing surface ready, with markers or other writing instruments;
- providing Bibles, paper, and pens and pencils for group members who may need them.

Finally, be sure to set aside time within this session to follow up on the "homework" of undertaking the spiritual gifts assessment (see "Spiritual Gifts" later in this session).

As your fellow group members arrive, thank each for her or his participation in this study, direct them to the refreshment table, and then invite them to sit down and prepare for conversation.

Welcome and Opening Prayer

At the time announced for the beginning of the session, welcome the participants to this fourth session in the *Make a Difference* study. Again, express appreciation for the participants' presence and commitment to the study. Ask if any participant would like to open the session with prayer, and if so, encourage that person or persons to do so. If no one volunteers, you might offer this prayer on behalf of the group:

Gracious and ever-loving God: You have created us to live in community, to live together in genuine fellowship with others, both near and far. As we explore the corporate dimensions of discipleship, open our eyes, our ears, and our minds to your presence with us, giving us the divine assurance that we are never alone, that your love, your grace, and your power surround us every moment of our lives. We offer this prayer in the name of Christ Jesus our Lord. Amen.

Invite a fellow participant to light the candle for your group in honor of someone who has made a difference in his or her life, embodying the spirit of this study. Ensure that each session gives someone different an opportunity to light the candle and lift up someone special. Ideally, everyone will have a chance to do this, although if you have more than six participants you will have to allow people to double up or find another creative solution.

If you feel it is appropriate, you might invite group members to consider what the lighting of the candle at the beginning of each session has meant to them, and how they can make use of this brief ritual in their own homes or with friends and family following this study.

View the Video

After your group has lit the candle, play the video for session 4 of the *Make a Difference* DVD. As always, be prepared to stop the video when any participant wishes to see or hear something on the video again. After the video session ends, discuss using the following questions:

Ask: What did you see or hear on the video that emphasizes the communal nature of the Christian faith?

Ask: How does the video conversation help you to imagine how to live out Christian community in ways you might not have thought about before?

Ask: : In the video, Nick and Lisa mention that people in churches today struggle to connect deeply with one another. How could we embrace and strengthen our connections with other Christians?

Engage

Continue exploring the role of Christian community by stating the old but true cliché: "You can't be Christian alone." Ask group members to spend three minutes (time them) thinking about the meaning of this cliché, writing down everything that comes to mind when they consider it. Then discuss the meaning of the statement as a group.

Ask: Do all of us agree on the meaning of the statement "You can't be Christian alone?" Why or why not?

Ask: What did this idea mean in New Testament times? What has it meant throughout the history of Christianity?

Ask: To what extent does the statement mean something different now, in today's world?

Invite the group to consider the five bullet points at the beginning of chapter 4 of *Make a Difference*, on page 86. Ask a volunteer to read this list aloud, pausing after each bullet point. After each bullet point has been read, invite your fellow group members to raise their hands if this statement applies to them. Choose one person who raises his or her hand, and ask that person to clarify why the statement resonated with them. After all five bullet points have been read, discuss the following questions:

Ask: How does fellowship with others help ease the burden of attempting to make a difference for the transformation of the world?

Ask: What practical or spiritual benefits come from having a partner in mission or service?

Ask: What could you gain from a deeper, stronger Christian fellowship right now?

Biblical Companions

Remind your fellow group members about the biblical examples of women and men who discovered the value of support from others: Shiphrah and Puah, Moses, Jesus' seventy-two followers, and the early Christian apostles. See *Make a Difference*, pages 88–91, for reference.

Ask: What other examples can you think of from Scripture where people called to a difficult task found support or assistance by others who joined their efforts?

Ask: In these instances, who among the people involved heard God's call? How do you know? How did God call each person? What does this say about the way God calls and works through people?

Ask: As you think about ways you might make a difference in the world, ways in which God might be calling you, who else will need to come alongside you? Or whom are you being called to come alongside?

Do the Good Stuff

Invite the group to turn to pages 92–93 in *Make a Difference*, to the section titled "Do the Good Stuff." Invite a volunteer to summarize this section, making reference to the Scripture quotation from Acts 2:42-47.

Ask: When you think of the Christian faith, what do you think of as "the good stuff"? What's the most exciting part of Christian community and action in the world for you?

Ask: What parts of the good stuff are impossible to do alone? Why?

Ask: Are we already doing some of this good stuff in our church? What shape does it take in our community? What do you see in this that you would describe as miraculous?

Ask: What might we do to engage in this good stuff more fully, either through strengthening what we already do or through starting something new?

(Un)Common

In *Make a Difference*, James Harnish offers three significant steps for engaging in active discipleship as a group: commit to an (un)common mission, observe an (un)common ritual, and practice an (un)common generosity (pages 93–105). Invite a volunteer to summarize what the author meant by each of these things.

Ask: How do our common mission, common rituals, and common practices of giving bind us together as disciples of Jesus Christ?

Ask: What is our church's mission statement? How does it draw us together to strengthen our relationships with one another? How does it inform the way we each individually experience God's call to make a difference?

Ask: What do you see in our celebration of the sacraments (baptism and communion) that shapes the way we serve in the world?

Ask: What does the author mean by adding the prefix (Un) within each of the three steps? What is uncommon about our mission, our rituals, or our generosity? Uncommon in comparison to what?

Ask: What would non-Christians say is uncommon about our church's mission, rituals, or generosity?

Spiritual Gifts

Before you look to this week's "Action Ideas," take some time to discuss the Spiritual Gifts assessment that each person took on his or her own after your last session. Invite each group member to briefly share the results of his or her spiritual gifts assessment. Affirm these gifts, saying how you see these gifts in that person. Then invite discussion around the following questions:

Ask: What did you learn about yourself that you didn't know before as a result of this spiritual gifts assessment?

Ask: How did this exercise confirm what you already knew, or suspected, about the talents and gifts that you have that God has nurtured in you?

Ask: What unique opportunities to make a difference do you see now that these gifts have been identified in you?

Ask: Consider these gifts alongside the needs you see around you, whether in our community or among individuals you know. How might God be calling you to use your gifts to respond to these needs?

Ask: How do your gifts complement the gifts of others in your group? What might we (or a group of us) undertake together that will require many of our spiritual gifts working in cooperation?

Take Action

Turn to page 109 in *Make a Difference* and examine the "Action Ideas" for chapter 4. Ask for a volunteer to read these action ideas aloud, and invite each person to choose one that he or she will commit to over the coming week.

Close the Session

Close this session with a prayer inviting the Holy Spirit to continue to guide you all in discovering and nurturing your spiritual gifts, opening your eyes to the ways in which you might use them in service of Christ and your neighbors. Ask Christ to bring other people into your lives whose gifts will complement and support your own, and to help you work together with them to make a world-transforming difference. After offering this prayer, lead your fellow group members in reciting Wesley's Covenant prayer, this time changing the singular pronouns (I and me) to plural pronouns (we and us):

Lord, make us what you will.
We put ourselves fully into your hands:
> *put us to doing, put us to suffering,*
> *let us be employed for you, or laid aside for you,*
> *let us be full, let us be empty,*
> *let us have all things, let us have nothing.*

We freely and with willing hearts
> *give it all to your pleasure and disposal.*[1]

---

1 Adapted from "Wesley's Covenant Service," *The United Methodist Book of Worship* (Nashville: The United Methodist Publishing House, 2016), 291.

INTO THE CRUCIBLE
OF PAIN AND HOPE

Overview

This session focuses on the reality of turmoil, disappointment, failure, and shattered dreams that may be encountered when striving to engage in active discipleship in the world. But at the same time, this chapter demonstrates the strength, the passion, the faith, and the confidence in God that comes from daring to serve and discovering the very presence of God in self-sacrificial service and discipleship. These insights come from the Scriptures, especially from the hymn in Philippians 2:5-11. As always, participants will have opportunities to reflect on their own experiences of discipleship and service.

Prepare

Prepare for this session as you have for the preceding sessions: read chapter 5 of *Make a Difference* and preview the video. Review the lesson plan for this session, and pray for your fellow group members and for yourself as a leader. Arrive at the meeting location and make it ready by attending to the following matters:

- Arrange the chairs and tables.
- Make sure that the DVD player and television or projector and screen are in place and working properly.
- Set up the refreshment table.
- Set up the markerboard or other writing surface, and provide markers.
- Set out the candle and a means of lighting it to begin your time together.
- Provide Bibles, paper, and pens and pencils for group members who may need them.
- Make a copy of *The United Methodist Hymnal* available for each participant. If you don't have enough copies, two or three will be able to share a single copy.

Welcome and Opening Prayer

Greet participants as they arrive, direct them to the refreshment table, then invite them to join the group at your table or in their chairs. As always, begin the session at the appointed time. By now, the participants will know that the sessions begin on time and conclude at a designated time.

Commence this session by inviting one of the participants to offer an opening prayer. Or you might offer this or a similar prayer:

Almighty God, as we grow in our commitment to respond to your claim on our lives by serving our sisters and brothers, we seek your presence, your power, and your peace. We trust your promises, we seek to live in your love, we claim the Christ as our Lord, and we invite you to be a part of and a blessing within our time together. We offer this and all our petitions and praises in the name of Christ our Lord. Amen.

Invite a fellow participant to light the candle for your group in honor of someone who has made a difference in his or her life, embodying the spirit of this study.

View the Video

Introduce the session 5 video for *Make a Difference*, reminding the participants that any one of them can ask to have a part of the video replayed. At the conclusion of the video, raise these questions for discussion by the whole group:

Ask: What new insights did you gain about pain and hope as you watched the video conversation?

Ask: Where did you see examples of pain and hope mentioned in the conversation?

Ask: Based on the video conversation and your own experience, what obstacles often prevent us from entering places of pain?

Ask: How does a life of service call us to enter into pain and experience it ourselves? What hope do we gain for ourselves by doing so, and what hope do we give to others by doing so?

Engage

In this chapter of *Make a Difference*, James Harnish makes clear that we are to bring hope into places of pain—experiencing a "bright sadness" in which we bear pain and yet abide in hope at the same time.

Invite the group to discuss the concept of hope.

> **Ask:** How is hope different from wishful thinking?

> **Ask:** What is the source of hope during times of great pain, such as in the aftermath of tragedy or loss? How does hope at such times differ from hope we experience more frequently?

> **Ask:** How can hope be a tool, a means to an end, or a solution?

For many years, a long, involved statement of the objective of Christian education in (then) Methodist churches ended with the phrase: "and abide in the Christian hope." Invite the group to discuss the meaning of the phrase "abide in the Christian hope."

> **Ask:** What is the Christian hope and how do persons abide or live in that hope?

> **Ask:** What are some of the assumptions about Christian hope that are necessary in order to abide in it?

> **Ask:** How is Christian hope either alike or different from, or both, hope in general? What is the source of Christian hope?

> **Ask:** Can persons choose to live in Christian hope? If they do so, how are their lives different as a result of such a choice?

Conclude this discussion of hope by inviting participants to complete this sentence: "To live in Christian hope is to..."

The Bright Sadness

Harnish indicates that one often encounters God and the very presence of God when ministering to those in great need. Ask the group to reflect on this observation and to relate their own experiences that verify it.

Ask: What examples did Harnish use to illustrate the ways we encounter God in places of pain or need?

Ask: Why do you think those experiences became an occasion for people to meet God? What does this say about God? About human beings?

Ask: Do these examples line up with your own personal experience? Why or why not? If so, when have you encountered God during a time of pain or need?

Ask: What places of pain exist in your community? How do you experience that pain and share in it?

Ask: Is it possible to proclaim hope and experience a "bright sadness" without sharing someone else's experience of pain, in a sense taking on that pain yourself? Why or why not?

Ask: How can you enter the crucible of pain and hope? What difference can you make by doing so? How will you be changed as a result?

Learning from Hymns

The journey to fulfillment in service is never without stumbling blocks and difficulties. Distribute copies of *The United Methodist Hymnal*, and ask participants to look at the first verse of the classic hymn "Are Ye Able," number 530. Read this first verse aloud as a whole group, then invite the participants to a moment of silent prayer in response to the hymn's question: "Are ye able...to be crucified with me?"... "Yea...to the death we follow thee."

Ask: We often understand such language as "be crucified with me" in symbolic terms, yet it points to the fact that we'll experience pain in following Jesus. What real pain does Christian discipleship call us to?

Another hymn of the church that reflects this challenge is the fourth verse of "Spirit of God," number 500 in *The United Methodist Hymnal*, culminating with the words "teach me the patience of unanswered prayer."

Ask: When have you experienced unanswered prayer? What pain came as a result of that situation?

Ask: How was your hope affected by this experience? Did it give you a chance to practice hope? Did your hope diminish? Did it grow?

As a group, ponder the declarations made in these hymns. If your group enjoys singing, invite all to join in one or both of these hymns if time permits.

Live with the Mind-set of Jesus

Finally, Harnish uses the classic hymn from Philippians 2:5-11 as an outline for sacrificial service. Invite a volunteer to read this Scripture passage, and invite another volunteer to summarize Harnish's comments on it in *Make a Difference*, pages 120–128. Harnish breaks the hymn down into three injunctions: get yourself out of the way, become a servant, and learn obedience. Read these aloud, and ask a volunteer to write them down on the markerboard or other surface.

Divide your group into three teams, and assign one of the injunctions to each team. Ask each team to consider their injunction and do the following:

1. Summarize it in their own words.
2. List some of the reasons why following this injunction is difficult or unpopular.
3. State how Jesus models this injunction—not just for his time, but for our time as well.

Allow about five minutes for teams to discuss on their own, and then bring them back together into the full group. Give each team an opportunity to report on what they discovered.

Ask: Why is it difficult to set aside our own interests, become a servant, and learn obedience?

Ask: Which of these is the most difficult in our society? Why?

Ask: How would you describe the mind-set of Jesus based on Philippians 2:5-11 and our discussion so far?

Ask: What would it mean for you to adopt the mind-set of Jesus with regard to other people or your community? What would you do, practically speaking, to become a servant? Who would you obey? Which of your own interests would you set aside?

Challenge group members to memorize Philippians 2:5-11. This brief passage—perhaps a very early Christian hymn—summarizes the mission of Jesus Christ and is a challenge to each Christian to uphold the three demands this passage makes of each one of us.

Into the Crucible

As a final activity, reflect on Harnish's title for this chapter. First, working as a whole group, define the word *crucible*. Then discuss the following questions briefly:

Ask: How and in what ways can active discipleship be likened to a crucible?

Ask: How can both pain and hope abide in the same crucible? What is the meaning of this pairing?

Ask: Do we have a choice of entering this crucible? Why or why not? What is the outcome if we choose to enter? What is the outcome if we refuse to enter the crucible?

Ask: How are you challenged and inspired to step into pain and hope?

Take Action

Invite group participants to turn to page 131 in *Make a Difference* and consider the "Questions for Reflection." Then invite the whole group to suggest additional questions they would like to explore. Ask a volunteer to read aloud the "Action Ideas." As usual, challenge each person to commit to one action idea that he or she may implement for the coming week. How will doing so inspire them to take a step toward making a difference for the transformation of the world?

Close the Session

Close this session with a time of silent prayer, then invite the participants to read aloud together the prayer with which Harnish closes this session (*Make a Difference*, pages 131–132).

FROM HERE TO KINGDOM COME

Overview

The thrust of this chapter is deceptively simple. It questions the prevailing notion that we are to escape from this world and replaces it with the assertion that we are called—working with God—to participate in the redemption of the world. Note the biblical references Harnish cites to support this view and the supporting evidence from leading thinkers and activists. As a result of discussing this chapter, participants will be invited to take part in a commissioning service. In it, each person will have an opportunity to silently pledge himself or herself to the continuing call of God to be engaged in active discipleship to make a true difference for the transformation of the world.

Prepare

Prepare for this session as you have for the preceding sessions, by reading chapter 6 of *Make a Difference* and previewing the video. Review the lesson plan for this session, and pray for your fellow group members by name. Don't forget to pray also for yourself, asking for God's guidance as you lead this study. Arrive at the meeting location and make it ready for your time together:

- Arrange the chairs and tables.
- Make sure that the DVD player and television or projector and screen are in place and working properly.
- Set up the refreshment table.
- Set up the candle at the center of your gathering space, and provide a way to light it.
- Set up the markerboard or other writing surface and provide markers.
- Provide Bibles, paper, and pens and pencils for group members who may need them.
- Allow time at the end to share a brief commissioning service, where you will confirm one another in your call to make a difference and go in the confidence of God's children.

Welcome and Opening Prayer

As you have throughout the study, welcome participants by name and invite them to the refreshment table before they find their way to their seats. Begin at the appointed time with this or a similar prayer:

Almighty God, you have called each of us live a life that makes a difference and seeks to shape the world according to your kingdom. Forgive our attempts to run from that call and to use false excuses for failing to live up to your summons. Make each of us instruments of your grace and peace in all that we do, and challenge us to be the agents of reconciliation, redemption, and renewal that you call us to be here and now. We offer this prayer in the name of Christ our Lord. Amen.

Invite a fellow participant to light the candle for your group in honor of someone who has made a difference in his or her life, ensuring that it is someone who has not yet had an opportunity to light the candle.

View the Video

After your group has lit the candle and opened in prayer, introduce and play the video for this session. As always, invite the participants to ask to have sections of the video replayed for clarification or amplification.

Ask: What key ideas or insights stood out to you as you watched the video conversation?

Ask: What does God's kingdom coming look like to you? What concrete, physical results do you think (or hope) it will bring about?

Ask: All of the speakers talked about mustard seeds. Where do you see mustard seeds, tiny seeds of God's kingdom, in your life or in our community?

Engage

The final chapter of *Make a Difference* is rich with images and ideas as Harnish shifts our focus toward anticipating the redemption of this world rather than seeking an escape from it. Ask all participants to turn to the section in the chapter with the heading "Begin with the End." Invite a volunteer to read aloud the first paragraph on page 135 which begins with the words "A more hopeful...". Invite the group to consider what it will mean for the whole world to be redeemed using the following questions:

Ask: What does the phrase "redemption of the world" mean to you?

Ask: What will a fully redeemed world look like? Describe this world in as much detail as possible. How do you arrive at this picture?

Ask: How is the idea of the redemption of this world different from the idea of going to heaven after we die? How does it change the way we behave in this life?

Ask: Can the whole world be redeemed? All of it?

Ask: What role do we human beings play in the redemption of the world?

Ask: What role can you as an individual play in the redemption of the world? What difference can you make? How?

The Ugliness of This World

Now ask one person to read the two statements from Archbishop Desmond Tutu on page 136 of *Make a Difference*. Ask each person to turn to his or her neighbor and discuss the following questions in response to these two statements:

- Tutu lists several pieces of evidence of what he calls "the ugliness of this world." What other evidence do you see as "ugliness" in the world?
- Is ugliness growing, or is it diminishing?

Allow each pair of participants to discuss for five minutes, then invite them to report to the whole group what they discussed.

Ask: What are human beings doing to make ugliness grow in the world? What are human beings doing to make ugliness diminish?

Ask: If we believe in the redemption of the world, then our future is one in which this ugliness is gone. What can we do to live this future in the present, living in a way that diminishes ugliness completely?

Anticipate Your Heaven Below

Refer the participants to the quotation from Charles Wesley to "anticipate your heaven below" on page 137 of *Make a Difference*. Harnish goes on to suggest that "to anticipate heaven is to live now in ways that bear witness to the way we believe the world will be when God's saving work is completed and God's redemption is accomplished." Invite the group to reflect on how Christians are called to live now in anticipation of heaven.

Ask: If we live in anticipation of heaven, what will have to change about your life?

Invite each participant to think of at least three changes she or he would have to make in his or her daily life in order to live as she or he believes the world will be when God has redeemed the world. Make sure everyone has a piece of paper and a pencil or pen, and ask each person to write down these three changes that he or she will have to make. Encourage participants to carry that piece of paper daily in their pocket or purse and to refer to it often, reflecting on the degree to which they are actively making these changes in daily life.

On pages 137–138 of *Make a Difference*, Harnish lists six areas in which committed disciples work in order to redeem the world. Ask for a volunteer to read these six areas aloud. Invite participants to list on a piece of paper those examples among the six in which they are already actively engaged, and to identify those others that captured their attention.

Remind the participants that this list of six is illustrative, not exhaustive. Ask participants to list other concerns that focus on a renewed creation and the redemption of the world with which they are involved or with which they may become involved.

Ask each participant to pray silently, then to choose one or more of these areas in which he or she could become more directly involved, giving with time, energy, or service in addition to monetary contributions.

Ask: What steps can you take in the next three days to make a difference in this area? In the next two weeks? In the next two months? In the next year?

Ask: How is your involvement in one or more of these areas already enriching your life while at the same time moving—perhaps ever so slowly—toward a redeemed world?

As a whole group, celebrate the involvement of group members in seeking to redeem all of creation.

Make a Big Difference in Little Things

Remind the group that some frustration will set in when Christians become excited about redeeming the world. Progress is painfully slow, and often steps seem to be going in the wrong direction. Draw everyone's attention to the sections in Harnish's chapter titled "Make a Big Difference in Little Things" and "Offer Your 'Stubborn Ounces'" (pages 141–143 and 145–147 in *Make a Difference*). Invite a volunteer to summarize these two sections.

Ask: What perspective does the idea of "stubborn ounces" give to our efforts to make a difference in the world? Do you find this perspective helpful? Why or why not?

Say: One of the great temptations facing those excited about the coming Kingdom is the desire to tackle the big problems or issues first. This was Peter's situation on the Mount of Transfiguration and again in the garden when Jesus was arrested. But Harnish points out clearly that none of us can begin at the top; the path to the top is through incremental small steps. We may not be able to have much influence on international policy, for instance, but we can feed our hungry neighbors and welcome the strangers as our sisters and brothers. To use a cliché, a journey of a thousand miles begins with a single step.

Ask: What is the single step that you can take to help move the world toward redemption? What is a small way that you can make a big difference?

Ask: Where will you place the "stubborn ounces" of your weight?

Take Action

Examine the "Questions for Reflection" and "Actions Ideas" for chapter 6, on pages 152–153 of *Make a Difference*. Invite each participant to identify at least one action idea to implement in the coming week.

Before you close the session, encourage the group to reflect on the six sessions of this study over the past several weeks.

Challenge each person to name one or two things that he or she has learned over the course of this study.

Ask each person to identify one way in which he or she has changed as a result of reading this book and participating in this study.

Finally, encourage each person to name one way in which she or he has become unsettled, uneasy, or uncomfortable as a result of reading this book and taking this study.

Ask: How might God be calling you to make a difference in a unique way, which only you can respond to?

Close the Session

As an act of commitment, invite the participants to join in an act of commissioning, designating themselves as those who will strive to take part—no matter how seemingly small the act—in the redemption of the world.

Invite the participants to form a circle. Remember that you are part of the circle. Ask the participants to respond to each of these questions and invitations as each person feels called:

Leader: God is calling each of us to be agents of change, to overcome the darkness with the light of Christ's love. Will you serve in such a way in your family, your community, and elsewhere?

The group responds: *Yes.*

Leader: Do you believe that God has called you to a specific ministry and witness, and that God will equip you to carry out that task?

The group responds: *Yes.*

Leader: Will you earnestly pray for one another as each seeks and initiates her or his specific ministries in the community and world?

The group responds: *Yes.*

Leader: Will you give God the glory for any and all progress and continue to view yourself as but a tool in the hands of a loving God?

The group responds: *Yes.*

Leader: Therefore know that God has commissioned you to the ministry of redemption and active discipleship, tasks you will not undertake alone but in the company of the Lord and like-minded disciples.

The group responds: *Thanks be to God!*

Conclude by saying the Lord's Prayer together.